A Dance
IN MY HEART

A Heartwarming
Picture Book to Remember
a Special Uncle

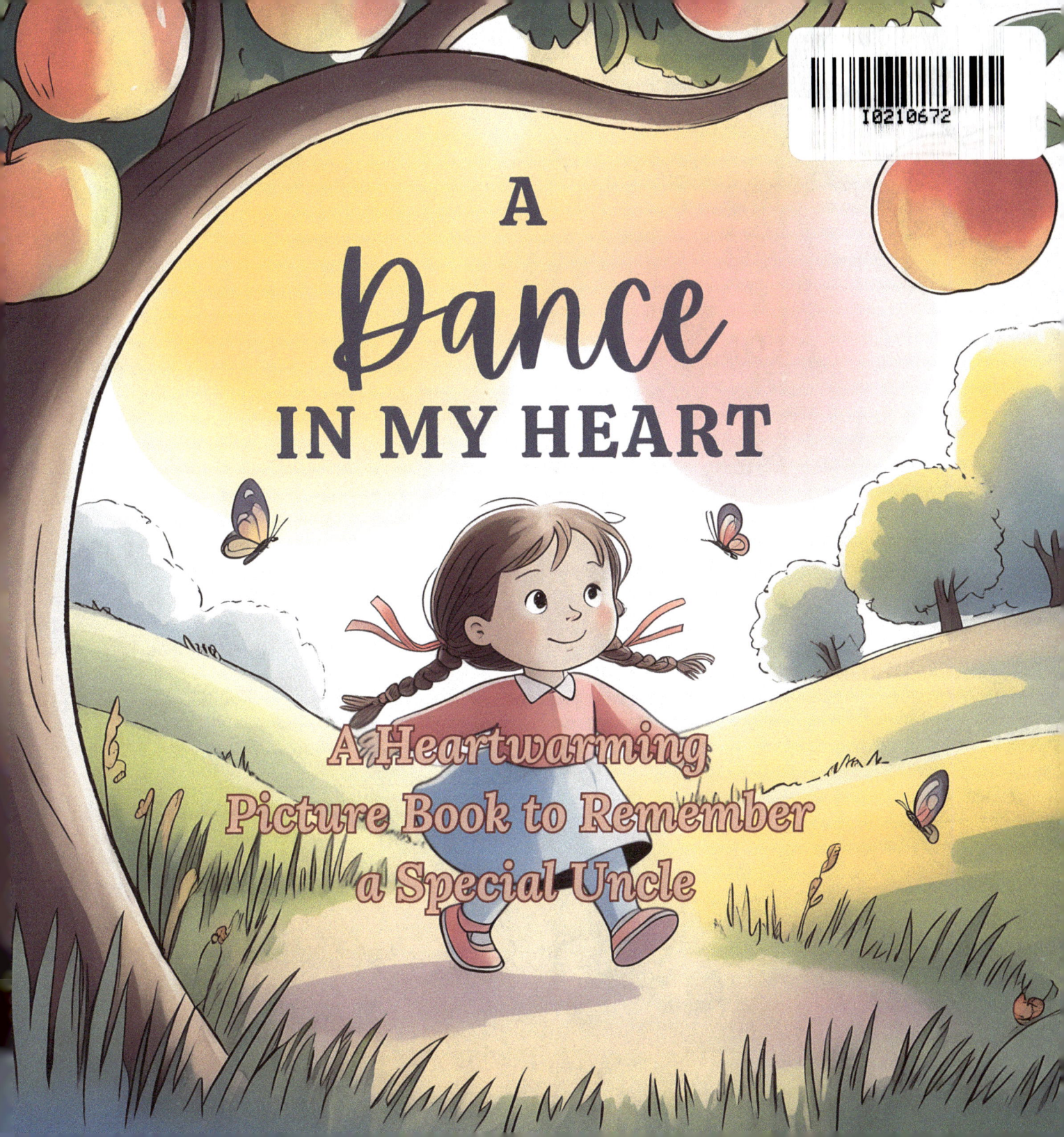

For every child who misses
someone they love.
May you always remember
the hugs,
the laughter,
and the love that still
dances in your heart.

Hi there, little one

This is a story about missing someone very special—like an uncle—and learning that even when someone is gone, their love can still stay with us. Sometimes our hearts feel big and stormy, and that's okay.

This book is here to help you feel safe, warm, and loved while you remember the happy times.

Let's take a gentle journey together.

Love,
Michelle

This Book Belongs to

_____

Written with Empathy and Care

this story reminds families
that saying goodbye
doesn't mean forgetting...
It means remembering
with love.

Book Cover by Tukotuku Publishing
Illustrations by Tukotuku Publishing
First edition 2025
Print ISBN:978-1-991366-38-2
Ebook ISBN:978-1-991366-39-9
michellehuirama.com

My Uncle Isn't Here Anymore

the house feels quieter without him.

Sometimes I miss his laugh so much it hurts.

Sometimes I close my eyes and hear it again.

uncle loved to dance in the kitchen.

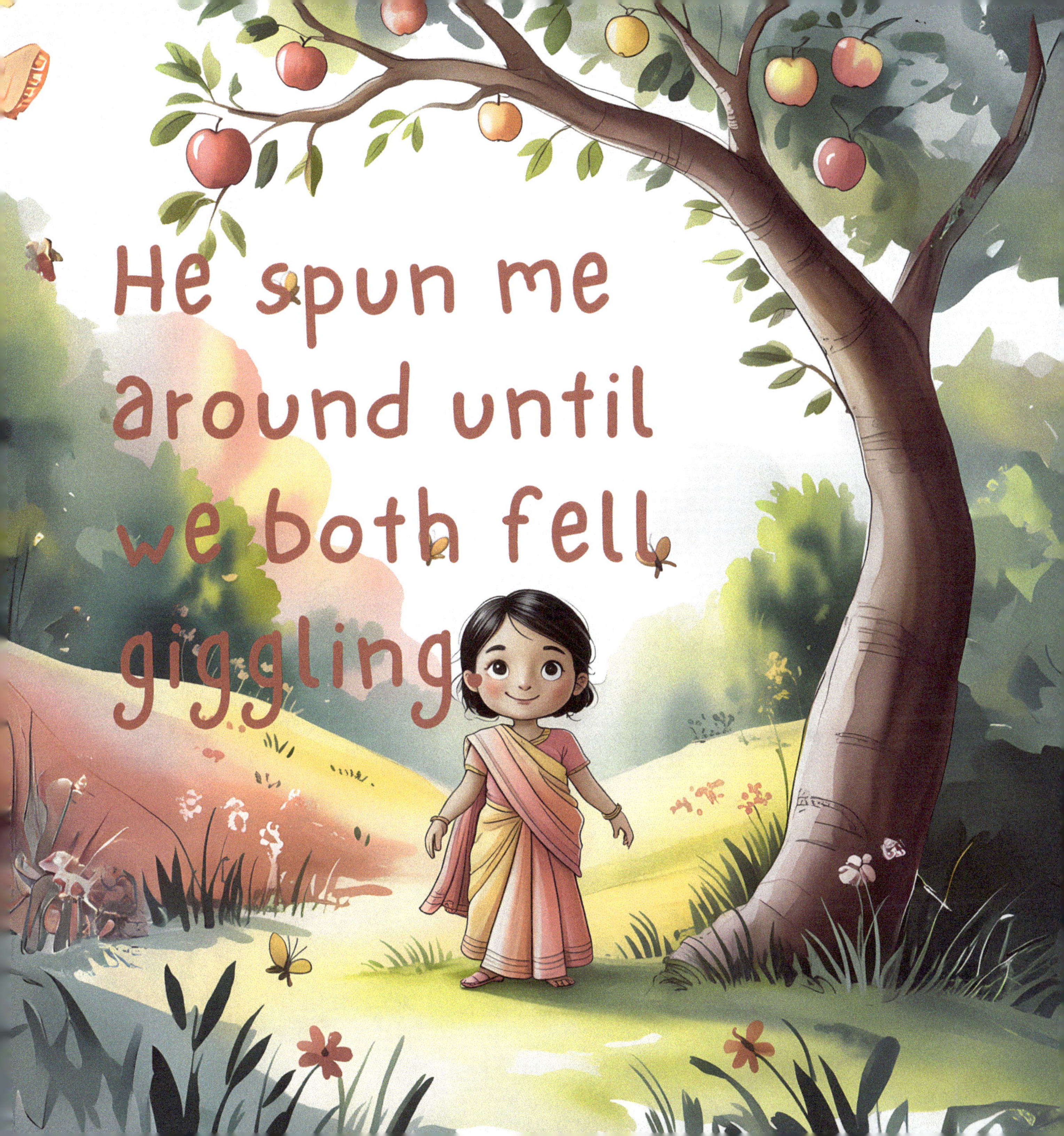

He spun me around until we both fell giggling.

He clapped to
the music and
tapped
his feet

His joy was a
song that filled
the room

Now the
music feels
far away.

My heart feels heavy, like it forgot the steps.

I wonder if I'll ever dance the same again.

But then I remember: Uncle's love is still here.

It hides in the stories he told.

It shines in
the silly faces
he made.

It whispers in
the lessons
he taught
me

It glows in
the hugs he gave

When I look at the stars, I see him smiling

When I hear
my favorite song,
I feel him dancing.

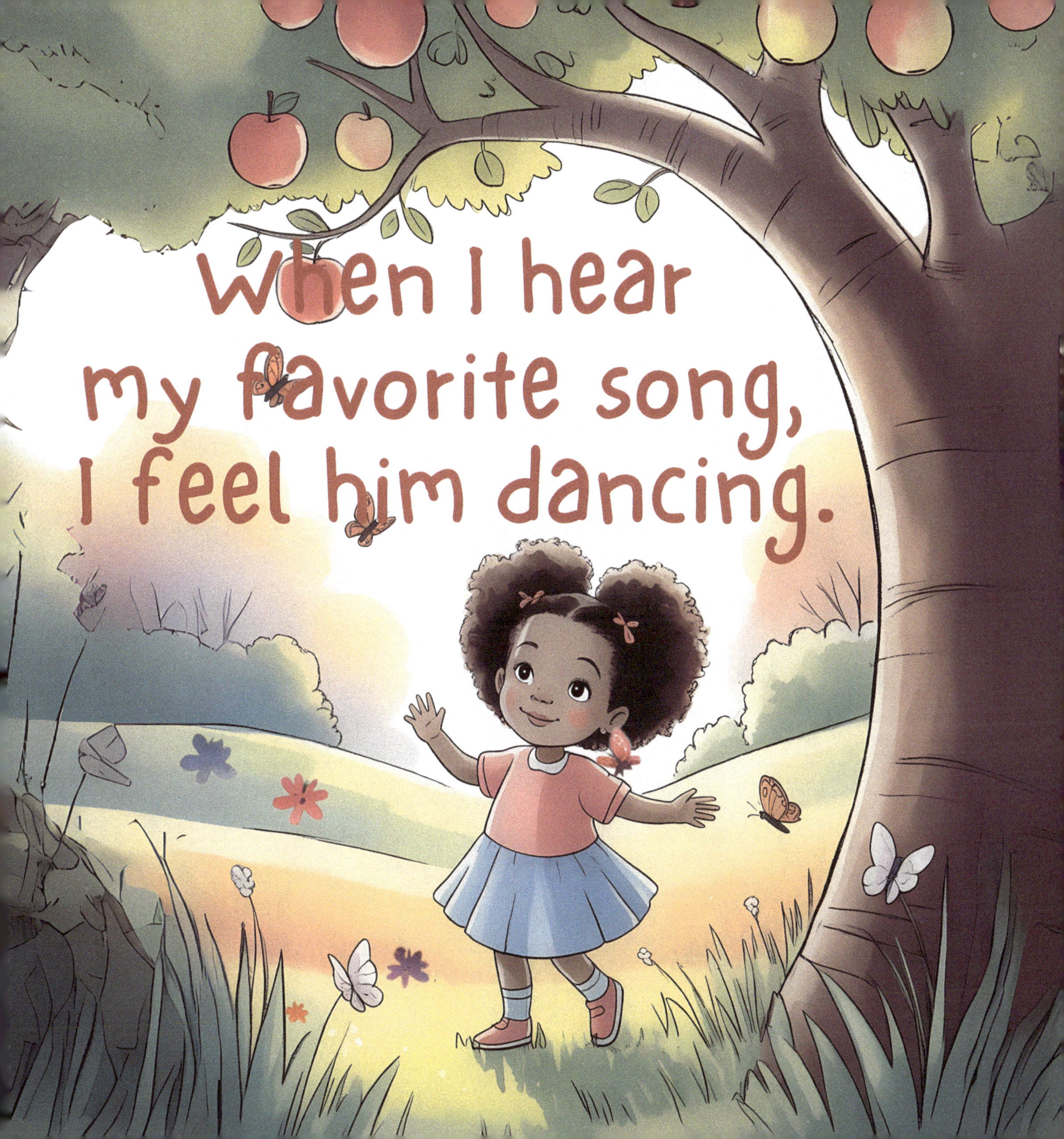

Love doesn't leave, even when people do.

I draw pictures of him on bright paper.

I write his name with sparkly crayons.

I tell Mom my favorite Uncle stories.

She tells me hers too.

We made a
memory box
together.

Inside, we put Uncle's photo.

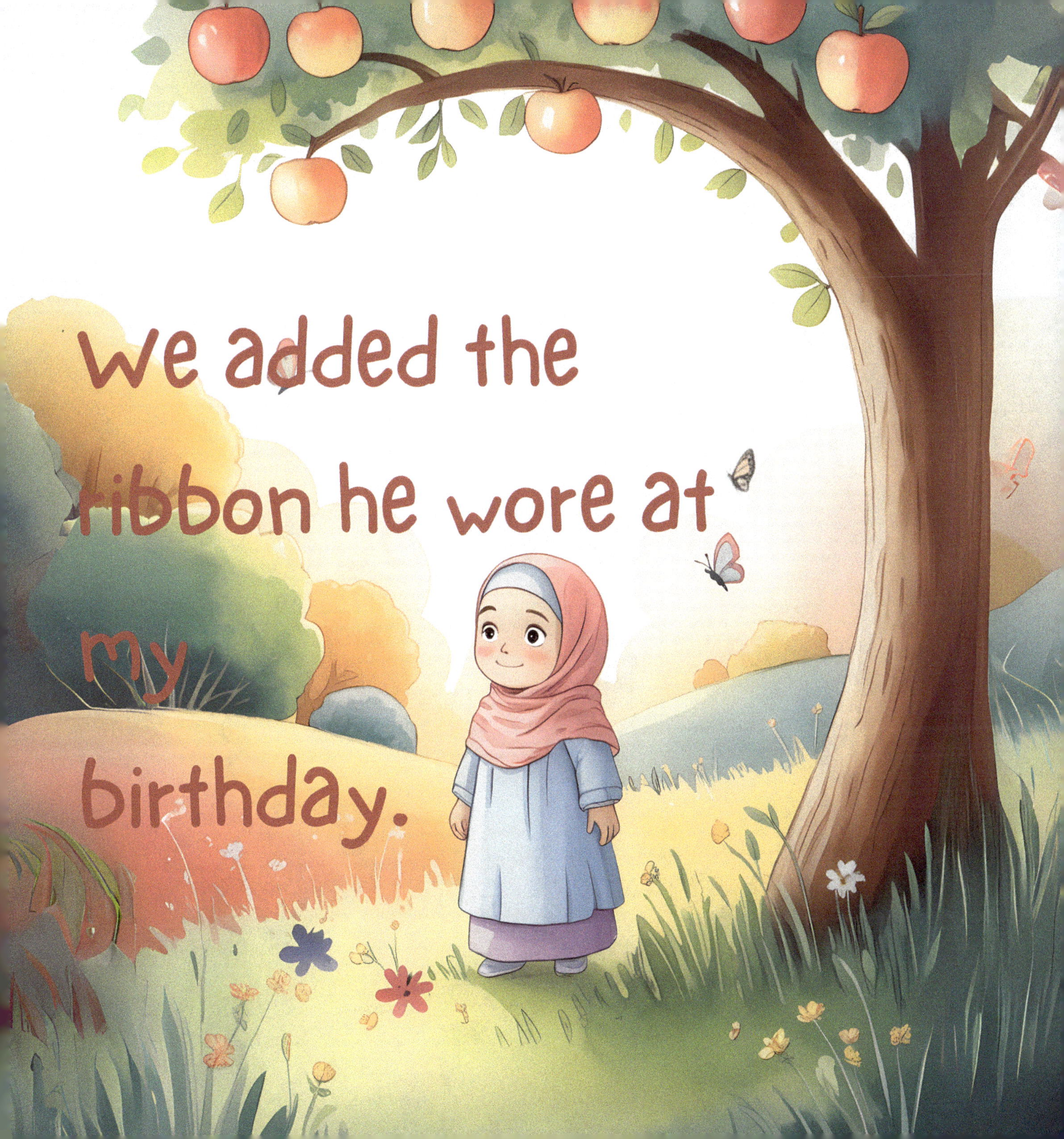

We added the ribbon he wore at my birthday.

And a little note
that said,
"I love you."

Some days I cry,
and that's okay..

Some days I smile, and that's okay too.

Healing is slow, like learning new dance steps

But every step brings uncle closer.

Now, when I dance
in the kitchen,
I feel him.

I spin and twirl and laugh for us both.

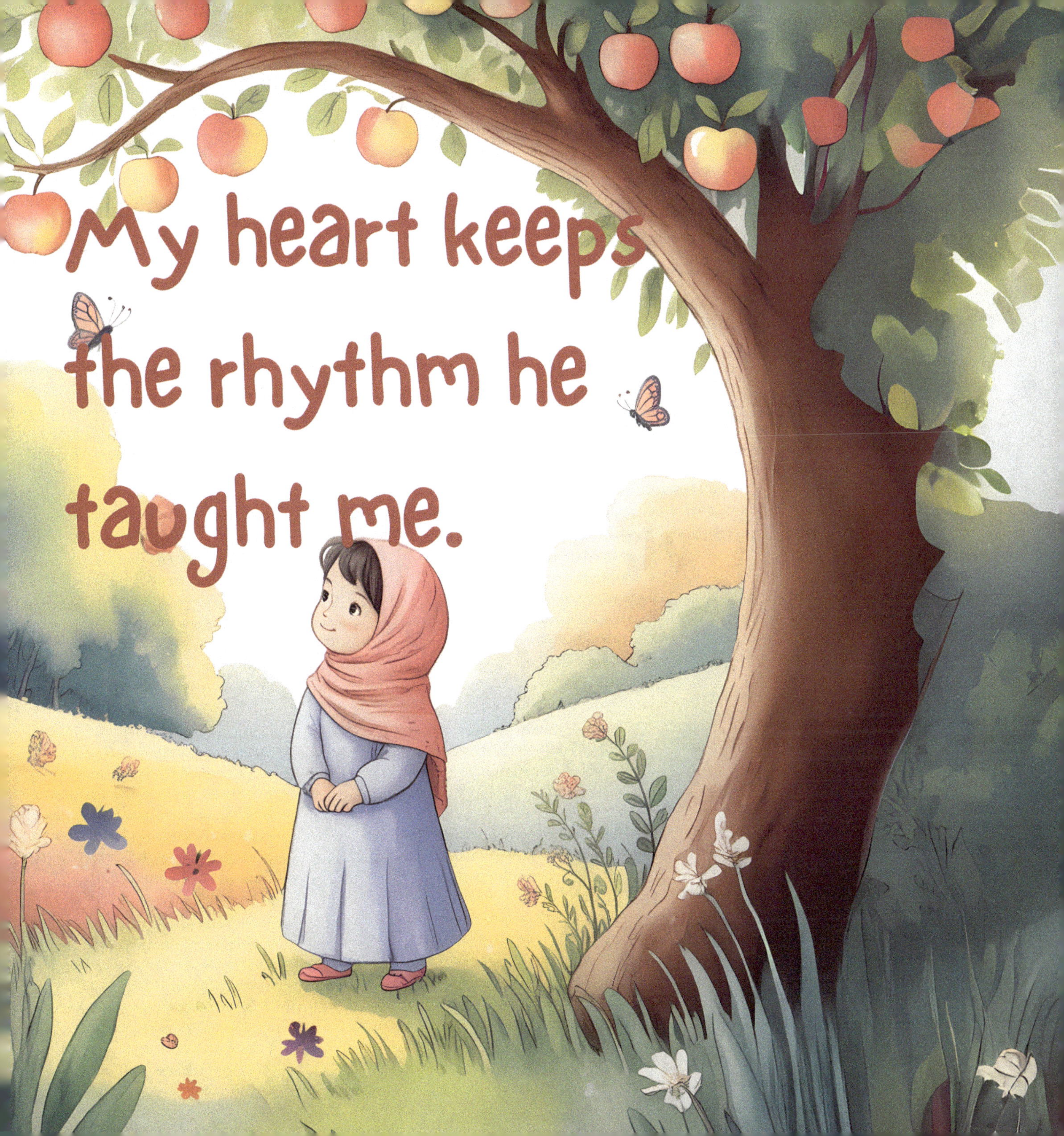

My heart keeps the rhythm he taught me.

Because uncle's love will always dance with me.

Let's Write a Note to Uncle

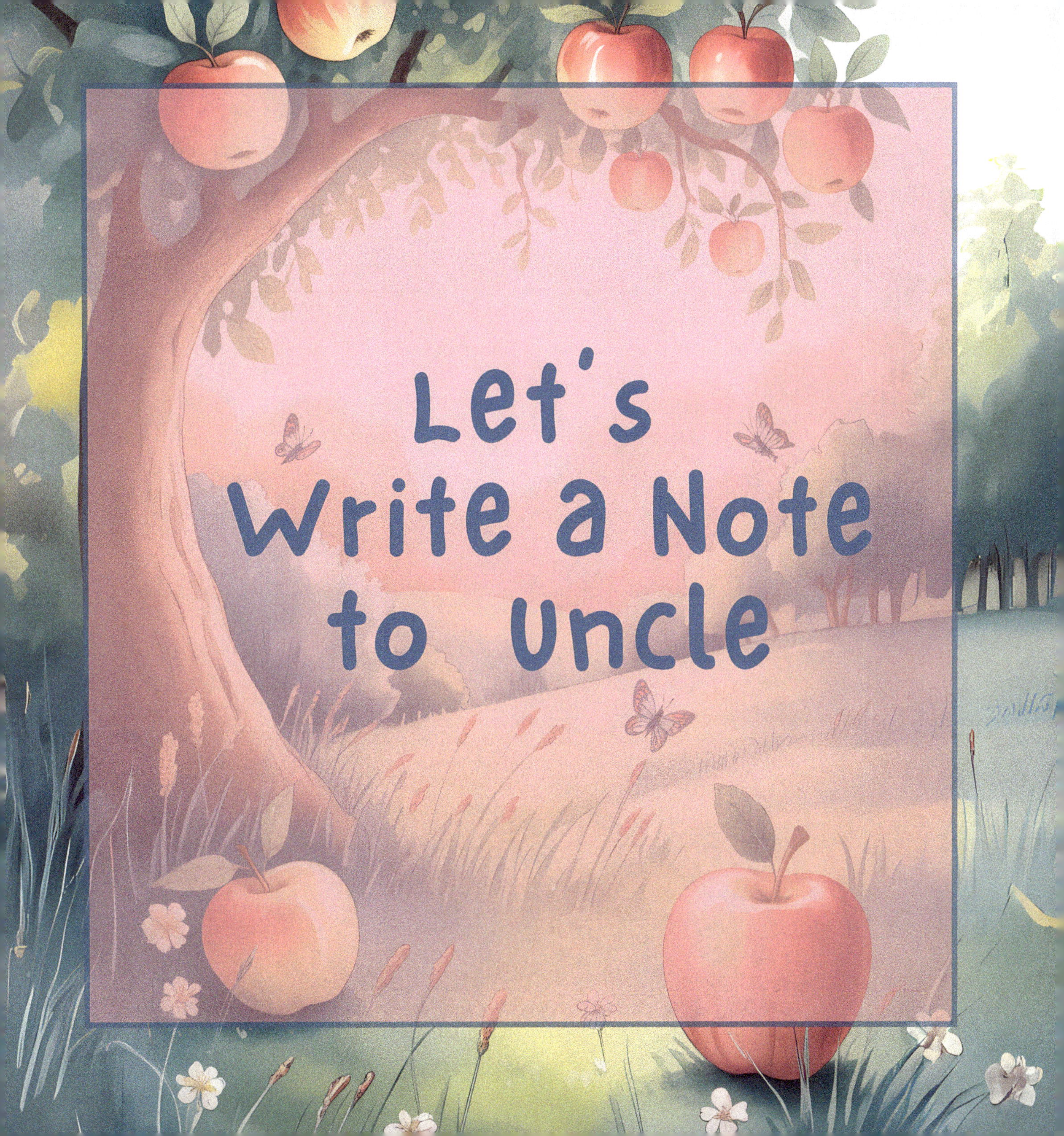

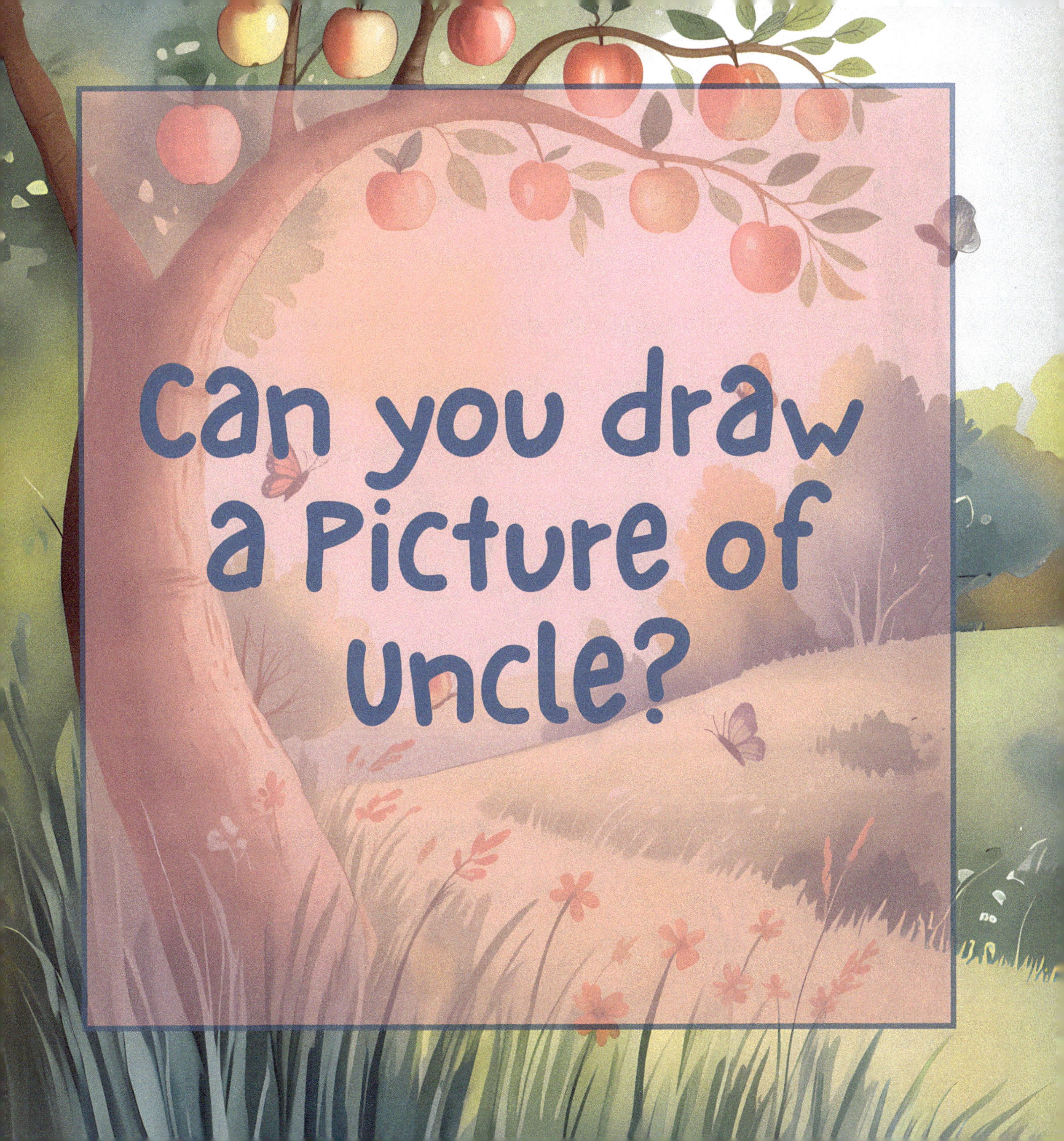

Can you draw a picture of Uncle?

Why not Draw A Favorite Memory that you have with Uncle

What would
you like
to tell uncle?

Draw a memory that makes you smile when you think of Uncle

Draw a memory that makes you smile when you think of Uncle

Draw a picture
of a happy memory
with
Uncle

Let's create your own story about Uncle. It can be happy, sad, funny, or all of those. start with "Once upoun A time....."

A Note for your Heart

When someone you love – like a uncle leaves you,

it can feel like your heart has a missing piece.

But little by little, as you remember the cuddles,

the playtimes, and the love you shared...

something amazing happens.

that missing piece becomes a memory,

and that memory becomes part of who you are.

Your heart grows.

And the love you gave –

and felt –

stays with you, always.

Wherever you go,

whatever you do,

your uncles's Smile

will walk beside you...

tucked safely in your heart.

THE END

A Note
for grown-ups

Create Space for Expression

Encourage creative outlets-drawing,

journaling,storytelling.
or even role-playing.
Let them choose how they'd like to honor
and remember their Uncle.

Supporting your Child through the loss of a Uncle

Losing an Uncle can often be a child's first experience with deep grief. It can bring up big feelings—sadness, confusion, even fear. A Dance in My Heart was created to gently help your child explore those emotions and begin the healing journey through love, memories, and creativity.

Here's how you can support them along the way:
Let them talk freely about Uncle and what they miss.
Encourage drawing, storytelling, or letter writing to express feelings.
Reassure them that all emotions are okay— there's no wrong way to grieve.
Share your own memories and feelings, showing that it's okay to feel and remember together.
This book is a soft space where your child can feel safe, loved, and reminded that even though Uncle is gone, his love still lives in their heart.

Validate their Feelings

Children may express sadness, anger, guilt, or even relief.
All of these are normal.
Let your child know it's okay to feel what they're feeling — and that grief doesn't have a timeline.
Say things like-

"I miss Uncle too." Let your child know it's okay to feel sad.
"I'm here for you."

Talk Honestly About Death

Use age appropriate language Avoid confusing phrases like "went to sleep" — instead, gently explain that all living beings have a life cycle. Honest conversations build trust and emotional resilience.

Rituals
Can Help

Creating a memory box,

planting a flower,

or holding a simple ceremony

can give children

a sense of closure and a tangible

way to say goodbye.

Model Healthy Grieving

If you're grieving it's okay to show it.
When children see you
sharing your emotions openly,
it reassures them that
sadness is part of love —
not something to hide..

Most importantly,
Their Uncle may be gone,
but the bond they shared
will always be part
of who they are.

with love,

Michelle

Even when someone we love
is no longer here,
their love doesn't vanish.
It moves gently,
like a dance in our heart.
Strong. Joyful. Always there.
This story is for every child
who misses their uncle—
the one who made you laugh,
who showed you new tricks,
who held you close
and loved you big.
Even though you can't see him now,
his love still dances inside you.
This is your heart-dance.
And it will never fade.

This Book is part of a gentle
grief series called
"Hearts that Remember" and
is for little ones who are
learning
to love, lose,
and remember

Let's meet
Michelle Huirama

Hi! I'm Michelle, and I write gentle picture books for little ones learning about big feelings.
When my own loved ones passed away, I wished there had been a soft, simple story I could read to the children in my life—something that would help them feel safe, loved, and less alone. That's why I wrote A Dance in My Heart. It's a gentle hug in book form, made to help children understand grief and remember the love that never goes away.
I believe even the smallest hearts deserve stories that bring light during dark times. I hope this book brings comfort to your family and helps keep Uncle's love shining bright.

Ko Tukotuku te Reikura
Ko Tamainupo te Hapu
Ko Karioi te Maunga
Ko Waikato te Ipukarea
Ko Tainui te Waka